ESSENTIAL FITNESS

STRENGTH TRAINING

BY SARAH ROGGIO

An Imprint of Abdo Publishing
abdobooks.com

ABDOBOOKS.COM
Published by Abdo Publishing, a division of ABDO, PO Box 398166, Minneapolis, Minnesota 55439.

Printed in the United States of America, North Mankato, Minnesota.
052024
092024

Cover Photo: iStockphoto
Interior Photos: Westend61 GmbH/Alamy, 2–3, 68; Shutterstock Images, 4–5, 11, 14, 23, 33, 35, 48, 55, 57, 61, 71, 72, 75, 78, 84, 93, 100–101; Igor Shootov/Shutterstock Images, 7; iStockphoto, 8, 10, 13, 34, 51, 62, 80, 95; Desmond Morris Collection/World History Archive/Alamy, 17; Bob Riha Jr./Archive Photos/Getty Images, 18; Daxiao Productions/Shutterstock Images, 24; Ezra Shaw/Getty Images for Ironman/Getty Images Sport/Getty Images, 26–27; Tok Anas/Shutterstock Images, 29; Ibra Shoot/Shutterstock Images, 30; Tyler Olson/Shutterstock Images, 37; Yuichi Masuda/Getty Images Sport/Getty Images, 38–39; Marlin Levison/Star Tribune/Getty Images, 41; Yuri Arcurs/Alamy, 42–43; Joan Cros/NurPhoto/Getty Images, 43; Carlos Calixto Rayo Bravo/Shutterstock Images, 44; Christa Boaz/iStockphoto, 47; David Cannon/David Cannon Collection/Getty Images, 52–53; Vladimir Sukhachev/Shutterstock Images, 58; Minerva Studio/Shutterstock Images, 60; Perry Knotts/Getty Images Sport/Getty Images, 64–65; Stratford Productions/Shutterstock Images, 67; Tim Clayton/Corbis Sport/Getty Images, 76–77; Petri Oeschger/Moment/Getty Images, 83; Max Kegfire/Shutterstock Images, 87; Leonid Kos/iStockphoto, 88; Alex Bogatyrev/Shutterstock Images, 89; Laurence Griffiths/Getty Images Sport/Getty Images, 90–91; Jacob Lund/Alamy, 94–95; Dragana Gordic/Shutterstock Images, 98

Editors: Charlie Beattie and Christa Kelly
Series Designer: Jake Slavik

Library of Congress Control Number: 2023949544

PUBLISHER'S CATALOGING-IN-PUBLICATION DATA
Names: Roggio, Sarah, author.
Title: Strength training / by Sarah Roggio
Description: Minneapolis, Minnesota: Abdo Publishing, 2025 | Series: Essential fitness | Includes online resources and index.
Identifiers: ISBN 9781098293307 (lib. bdg.) | ISBN 9798384912576 (ebook)
Subjects: LCSH: Weight training--Juvenile literature. | Bodybuilding--Juvenile literature. | Muscles--Juvenile literature. | Exercise--Juvenile literature. | Physical fitness--Juvenile literature.
Classification: DDC 613.71--dc23

CONTENTS

481

SAILING STRONG

Mia beamed at her friend Simone as they walked along the dock. They had spent several summer camp seasons sailing the small Optimist starter boats. But today was a big day. They were finally getting a chance to sail the larger Club 420 (C420) racing boats.

"Goodbye, bathtub boats," Mia said as they passed the 7.8-foot (2.4 m) Optimists, which looked like tiny rowboats.[1] "On to the real deal!"

Instead of having a single sail like the Optimists, the 13.8-foot (4.2 m) C420s had two sails.[2] Simone and Mia would get to sail together in the C420 like a racing team. They had already decided that Mia would steer, and Simone would handle most of the sail adjustments. They were both eager to train for the C420 racing team tryouts at the end

Strength training can be valuable for any sport.

of the summer. Simone and Mia attached the sails to their boat as they had been taught and rolled the boat on its wheeled trailer down the ramp and into the water.

"This is so cool!" Mia shouted as she grabbed the aluminum tiller. She pushed and pulled the tiller to turn the boat. Each time the boat changed direction, she and Simone ducked under the metal boom holding up the main sail as it swung to the other side of the boat. They then hopped up to sit on the edge of the boat. That way they could balance the C420 against the force of the wind.

Mia and Simone tucked their feet under a strap on the bottom of the boat to keep it level. They stretched their legs and leaned back to move their body weight out over the edge of the boat. Mia's legs started trembling. After an hour-long class of steering and helping Simone pull on the ropes to adjust the sails, Mia felt like all her muscles were on fire. She sighed in relief when they

MAJOR MUSCLE GROUPS

Humans have more than 600 muscles. There are six main muscle groups: the chest, back, arms, abdominals, legs, and shoulders. Different exercises target different muscle groups, though because muscles work together so often, most exercises target multiple groups at once. Some experts advise training different muscle groups on different days. This gives each muscle group a chance to recover after a workout.

Balancing a boat against the force of the wind helps to keep it level and maintain speed.

finally docked before realizing that she and Simone still had to haul their boat out of the water.

Mia and Simone struggled to get the C420 onto the trailer. They eventually had to ask a classmate for help pulling the trailer up the ramp. Mia felt discouraged at how exhausted she was after operating the C420. How could they become serious racers like their hero, fellow teenage racer Merritt Sellers, if they weren't even strong enough to handle one day on the water? Merritt could handle a boat like this on her own!

"We have to get stronger, Simone," Mia said.

Simone nodded. "Let's ask Coach Roberts if we can join his racing team workouts."

The next morning, Mia's dad dropped her off at sailing camp an hour before her class.

Sit-ups are a common part of many strength workouts.

"Girl power!" he said, holding up his hand for a high five.

Mia rolled her eyes but smiled. "Thanks, Dad," she said as she slapped his hand. She turned around and ran to where Coach Roberts and the racing team were waiting.

"Today we're going to do sit-ups, lunges, and push-ups," Coach Roberts said.

Mia raised her hand. "What about weight lifting?" she asked. "Don't we need that to get strong?"

Coach Roberts shook his head. "We can add weights later, but all you need to build strength is some form of resistance. Using your own body weight is a great way to start. Let's begin today's workout. For our warm-up, we're going for a ten-minute jog."

Mia felt her heart rate increase as they jogged. "Are you . . . almost out of breath already?" she asked Simone.

"Yes . . . I . . . am!" Simone answered.

As she slowly adjusted to the exertion, Mia realized she was feeling good. It felt like the rush she got from sailing. After their run, Mia and Simone took small sips from their water bottles. They knew from sailing that it was important to stay hydrated during physical activity.

"OK, time for your first strength training exercise," Coach Roberts said. "Let's start small with one set of ten sit-ups."

Mia and Simone set their yoga mats down on the grass and then lay down on their backs. Mia felt her stomach muscles contract as she lifted her head toward her bent knees. They followed Coach's advice to fold their arms across their chest rather than

WARMING UP AND COOLING DOWN

Before exercising, it is important to transition the body from a resting state and prepare it for strenuous activity. A light warm-up of stretching and low-intensity exercise is a good way to increase a person's heart rate and body temperature, which warms and loosens muscles. Likewise, a cooldown is necessary once strenuous exercise is complete. By lowering the intensity, a person's heart rate, temperature, and breathing can slowly return to normal. This helps muscles recover.

risk hurting their necks by pulling their heads up with their hands. While they worked out, Coach explained that sit-ups would help strengthen their abdominal muscles so they would have better core stability.

Next, it was time for two sets of forward lunges. Mia and Simone stood next to each other and took a long step forward with their right feet. Coach told them to keep their backs straight as they bent their knees and lowered their bodies toward the ground. Mia felt the power of her right leg pushing her body up each time she returned to the starting point. After ten lunges, they put their left feet forward and did ten more lunges.

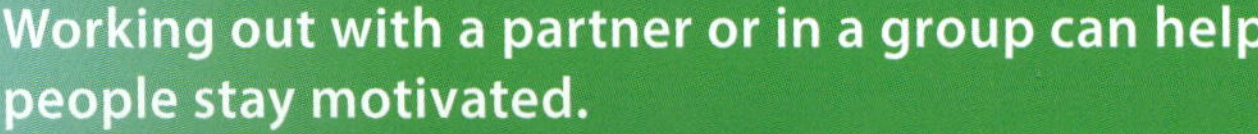

Working out with a partner or in a group can help people stay motivated.

Post-workout stretching can help prevent soreness and injuries.

Coach explained that lunges would help strengthen their thigh, glute, and calf muscles as well as improve their overall balance.

Finally, they finished with one set of ten push-ups. Mia and Simone got on all fours on their yoga mats, then extended their legs to balance their bodies on their hands and toes. They followed Coach's advice to contract their abdominals to keep their bodies in a straight line. Mia felt her arm and chest muscles contract each time she pushed herself up from the ground. Coach explained that push-ups would help strengthen their arm and chest muscles while protecting their shoulders from injury.

STRENGTH TRAINING GEAR

Though strength training can be done using only body weight, many athletes use tools to help them during their workouts. Weights are one such tool. Free weights can increase an exercise's difficulty. Other athletes prefer to use a weight machine. Resistance bands are also popular tools. These are stretchable elastic bands that help athletes contract their muscles. Plyometric boxes are commonly used during leg workouts. These boxes are often used for jumping exercises, but they can also be used for dips, lunges, and other movements.

They finished their strength training session with a ten-minute set of stretches that Coach called a cooldown. Mia was surprised at how good she felt. Her muscles didn't even feel sore. "Are you sure this will make us strong, Coach?"

Coach Roberts laughed. "It just takes a little work to make big changes. You'll see."

Coach Roberts was right. For the next few months, Mia and Simone joined the racing team for strength training sessions three times a week. Halfway through the summer, they added light weights to their workouts. Coach Roberts showed them the proper weight-lifting techniques to avoid injuries. Coach Roberts had told them that rest was also important. It would allow their muscles to rebuild and recover.

By the end of the summer, Mia felt powerful and proud. She and Simone could easily handle both racing the boat and hauling it out of the water. Finally, the day of the racing team tryouts arrived. Mia was nervous, but she remembered the mental strength tips from Coach Roberts. She took a deep breath, smiled, and visualized performing all the racing maneuvers perfectly.

Out on the water, Mia felt like she and Simone had become an amazing team. Working out together had not only made them physically stronger but more in sync as well. When a big gust of wind hit, they knew just what to do. They now had the strength and agility to adjust the sails and lean out over the water for as long as they needed to keep the boat under control. Mia laughed as the spray hit her face. She felt like she and Simone were already racing pros. When they returned to the dock, Coach Roberts confirmed that they were well on their way—they had made the team!

Sports such as sailing require strong arm, leg, and core muscles.

CHAPTER

WHAT IS STRENGTH TRAINING?

The term *strength training* often conjures images of bodybuilders with bulging biceps. But people don't need to bench-press to build strength. Lifting heavy books and jumping rope are both examples of strength training. Sometimes called resistance training, strength training is any exercise that makes the muscles contract against some type of opposing force. This could include body-weight exercises such as push-ups, lunges, and sit-ups that make the body work against gravity.

Strength training, like bodybuilding, can involve lifting weights. But the goals of strength training and bodybuilding are different.

The main goal of strength training is to build and maintain muscles.

The purpose of bodybuilding is to build *bigger* muscles, while the purpose of strength training is to build *stronger* muscles. Stronger muscles give someone the power to perform both everyday tasks and athletic feats. Some athletes also add mental strength training exercises to their routines. Mental strength training can help people focus, feel better about themselves, and reduce stress.

Arnold Schwarzenegger is a famous bodybuilder and actor. He acknowledged that strength is not all about lifting weights. According to Schwarzenegger, "The resistance that you fight physically in the gym and the resistance that you fight in life can only build a strong character."[1]

THE HISTORY OF STRENGTH TRAINING

Humans have been seeking ways to increase their physical strength for centuries. About 8,000 years ago in ancient China, men lifted rocks, metal objects, and swords to demonstrate their physical strength and fighting power. They even participated in ancient versions of weight-lifting competitions, hoisting huge bronze cauldrons that weighed hundreds of pounds.

Ancient Egyptians added heavy bags of sand to their weight-lifting routines, while people in ancient India swung wooden clubs to build strength. More than 2,000 years ago in ancient Greece, a renowned wrestler

Cauldrons lifted by ancient Chinese weight lifters were called dings. They were also used for cooking and for heating homes.

named Milo of Croton supposedly turned to animals for his weight training. According to legend, Milo lifted a calf every day from its birth until it grew into a full-sized adult ox. He also is said to have carried an ox on his shoulders at the stadium in Olympia, Greece, the site of the original Olympic Games.

In addition to filming his television show, Jack LaLanne published more than 20 books on exercise and dieting.

Today, people use modern weights and weight training machines to build strength. The United States has more than 115,000 gyms, health clubs, and fitness centers where people can go for strength training.[2] Health experts recommend that people strength train two to three days per week. Professional athletes, fitness experts, and celebrities often promote strength training exercises and courses.

Though strength training is now a normal part of modern fitness, this was not always the case. Jack LaLanne was among the first to change people's perceptions on strength training. As a teen, LaLanne built muscle by lifting weights and went on to become a champion wrestler. But when he decided to open a fitness center with spaces for patrons to lift weights, he was criticized and ridiculed.

NORA LANGDON

After a 35-year career in real estate, Nora Langdon started lifting weights at age 65. After her trainer encouraged her to enter a powerlifting tournament, Langdon went on to become a world champion powerlifter. In 2023, the Michigan retiree could bench press more than 200 pounds (90 kg). She could also both squat and deadlift 415 pounds (188 kg). "People often look at me and say, 'Oh, she won't be able to lift that.' I like surprising them," Langdon said.[4]

"People thought I was a charlatan," LaLanne said. "The doctors were against me—they said that working out with weights would give people everything from heart attacks to hemorrhoids."[3]

It wasn't just doctors who were wary of weight training at the time. Many coaches banned athletes from lifting weights because they thought building muscles would make athletes slow. But LaLanne helped change the public's mind through his exercise television program *The Jack LaLanne Show*, which debuted in 1951. Over the next 34 years, LaLanne taught millions of people how to strength train using weights, resistance bands, and body-weight exercises such as push-ups.

LaLanne also invented weight machines that people still use today for strength training, including leg extension and squat machines. The leg extension machine works the quadricep muscles (quads) on the front of the thigh. The squat machine works the quads, the gluteus muscles (glutes) in the buttocks, and the hamstring muscles along the back of the thigh.

ARTHUR JONES

After joining the US Navy in 1941, Arthur Jones became interested in weight lifting. He soon decided that free weights weren't challenging enough and that he would build his own weight machine. He exhibited the Nautilus at a 1970 bodybuilding competition and began selling the machines soon after. He went on to write fitness books and invent his own training regimen. Jones helped make weight training popular among everyday gym-goers at a time when it was done mostly by bodybuilders.

When LaLanne started out, he also encouraged exercise for people who typically weren't included in such messages, such as women, the elderly, and people with physical disabilities. He was particularly outspoken about providing fitness opportunities for the elderly and promoted the idea that people could stay strong for life.

To prove his point, even as LaLanne aged, he continued to perform great feats of strength. When he was 40, LaLanne put on 140 pounds (60 kg) of equipment and swam the entire length of San Francisco's Golden

Gate Bridge.[5] He did so to prove he wasn't too old to exercise. He also worked out with weights well into his 80s and continued to exercise nearly every day until his death in 2011 at age 96.

In 1968, Schwarzenegger found out just how seriously LaLanne took his own advice to stay physically fit. At age 21, after becoming the youngest winner of the Mr. Universe bodybuilding competition, Schwarzenegger agreed to a chin-up and push-up contest with the 54-year-old LaLanne. Schwarzenegger later recalled that LaLanne won easily.

YOUTH STRENGTH TRAINING

For many years, experts believed strength training would stunt children's growth. But today, most health experts believe that it is safe and beneficial for young people as well as adults. It can help young people stay active and prevent injuries. Many coaches now embrace strength training for their youth athletes as well. In addition, conditioning experts believe that strength training improves athletes' performance by enhancing their speed, agility, balance, and endurance.

Experts now say that kids can safely start strength training—including weight lifting—as soon as they're old enough to follow instructions. This could be as young as seven years old. Experts say that the keys to keeping weight lifting safe are to start out light, begin with a small number of repetitions, use proper form, and follow an expert's instructions.

STRENGTH TRAINING FOR WOMEN

Myths also persist about women's roles in fitness. Some people claim that women and girls are too weak to participate in strength training. Others claim that strength training is unladylike. Unfortunately, these myths have existed for thousands of years. In ancient Greece, women were not allowed to compete in the original Olympic Games. By the time the modern Olympic Games began in 1896, little had changed. Women were barred from competing in the Olympics until 1900.

Fifty years later, women in the United States began to challenge the idea that women should not engage in strenuous physical activity. Female fitness pioneer Lotte Berk was among the first to create a workout specifically for women.

ELAINE LALANNE

Jack LaLanne's widow, Elaine, continues to carry on his legacy. In 2023, Elaine was still working out at age 97. She starts every day with 20 minutes of exercises that include stretches, sit-ups, and hanging from a pull-up bar. "I've got a great core," she told *Muscle & Fitness* magazine.[6] She also co-authored the book *Pride & Discipline: The Legacy of Jack LaLanne* to help share her husband's physical feats and fitness philosophy.

Berk, a German dancer, created a strength training routine using the ballet barre, the handrail that dancers use for support while exercising. Berk's strength training technique became widely popular, and a fitness studio called The Bar Method was created to teach barre workouts. Today, people throughout the United States and Canada take classes at The Bar Method studios to build muscle.

In 1972, a federal law called Title IX also helped change perceptions about women and physical fitness. The law required public institutions to create equal opportunities for male and female athletes. It also meant

Barre workouts mix elements of ballet, Pilates, and yoga.

Many gyms focus exclusively on group classes that emphasize strength training.

that schools had to provide the same quality of weight and conditioning facilities for girls and boys.

Today's Olympic Games show that the world has come a long way in promoting equality for female athletes. In 2023, the International Olympic Committee (IOC) boasted that the 2024 Olympic Games would have an equal number of male and female athletes. The IOC had been inching toward this goal in the previous years, with

45.6 percent of competitors being female in the 2016 Olympic Games. That number jumped to 48.8 percent at the 2020 Olympic Games.[7]

COVID-19 AND STRENGTH TRAINING

Strength training gained popularity during the COVID-19 pandemic. With gyms closed due to lockdowns in 2020, many people were seeking ways to stay fit. Without access to gym weight machines and fitness classes, exercisers watched fitness videos online and did resistance band, free weight, and body-weight exercises at home.

The strength training trend continued. In 2022, the fitness app ClassPass reported a 94 percent increase in strength training classes from the previous year.[8] In 2023, the American College of Sports Medicine reported that strength training with free weights was the second-most popular fitness trend that year, followed by body-weight training in third place.[9]

Strength training has become so popular that some gyms are changing their layouts. In 2023, Planet Fitness cut back on space for cardio equipment such as treadmills to make more room for people to lift free weights and do body-weight exercises such as lunges, push-ups, and squats. "Strength training has become so much more widely embraced and accepted for all kinds of outcomes," *Fit Nation* author Natalia Mehlman Petrzela said in 2023.[10]

1%
BETTER

CHAPTER THREE

STRENGTH TRAINING AND THE BODY

Chris Nikic was born in 1999 with Down syndrome, a genetic condition that alters a person's development and causes low muscle tone. He was unable to walk on his own until age four because he struggled to balance. Nikic couldn't ride a bicycle until he was 15 years old.

In 2019, Nikic's father suggested that he start training for a race in the Ironman Triathlon series. The events require competitors to swim, bike, and run very long distances. If Nikic finished the grueling race, he would be the first person with Down syndrome to complete an Ironman and he might even make the *Guinness World Records*.

Fitness pioneer Chris Nikic, *left,* celebrates with fellow competitor Sebastien Bellin after the 2022 Ironman World Championships in Hawaii.

Nikic started small with a training schedule that his dad called 1 percent better. "When I first started training, the simple goal was to improve 1 percent in each exercise. I did one more lap of the pool, one more lap on the bike, and one more lap on the run every day," Nikic recalled. "When I was doing strength workouts, it would be one more pull-up, one more sit-up, one more press-up, and one more squat and barbell in the gym."[1]

Little by little, Nikic grew stronger. In 2020, at age 21, he completed a full Ironman Triathlon. The Florida competition required Nikic to swim 2.4 miles (3.9 km), bike 112 miles (180 km), and complete a 26.2-mile (42.2 km) marathon. *Guinness World Records* recognized his accomplishment after Nikic completed the race in 16 hours, 46 minutes, 9 seconds. He crossed the finish line just under the 17-hour cutoff time.[2]

THE SCIENCE OF STRENGTH TRAINING

Skeletal muscles are the muscles attached to the skeleton. These include the biceps, quadriceps, and pectorals. Exercise strengthens skeletal muscles by breaking them down. When people perform exercises such as weight lifting, they strain the fibers in their skeletal muscles, creating tiny tears. This trauma activates cells outside these muscle fibers to repair the damage. The body does this by producing new muscle fibers to replace damaged ones. This process is called *hypertrophy*. With proper rest and recovery, repeated hypertrophy makes muscles bigger and stronger.

Playing sports is the best way for young athletes to build muscle and stay fit, according to experts.

Nikic now serves as a Special Olympics ambassador. He also tours the country giving motivational speeches.

STRENGTH TRAINING GOALS

While strength training helped Nikic set a world record, athletes don't need to train like an Ironman to get strong. People can take small steps like Nikic did to meet their own strength training goals. The US Centers for Disease Control and Prevention (CDC) recommends that youth ages six to 17 years old do strength training exercises at least three days per week. These activities should be part

Strength training is most effective when the workouts are spread out, which allows muscles to rest and rebuild.

of the 60 minutes of daily exercise the CDC recommends for young people, rather than an additional task.[3]

To strengthen muscles, the CDC recommends that youth engage in activities such as playing sports, lifting weights, doing yoga, or working with resistance bands. It also recommends body-weight exercises such as pull-ups, push-ups, and planks. According to the organization, any activity that works the major muscle groups—arms, chest, shoulders, abdomen, back, hips, and legs—counts as a muscle-strengthening exercise.

To build healthy bones, the CDC recommends that people do exercises that involve impact with the ground. This impact puts force on bones, which makes them grow stronger. The organization categorizes running, gymnastics, and jumping rope as bone-strengthening exercises, as well as sports such as basketball, soccer, and tennis. These activities are especially important for youth as humans develop most of their bone mass by the end of adolescence.

As part of its Move Your Way campaign, a program launched in 2018 to encourage youth to be active, the Department of Health and Human Services asked teens to share videos about how they choose to get strong. "I feel better when I'm active, but I don't like going to the gym," one boy shared. "I think it's important to find an activity you like, something you can do after school. I like to play soccer with my brother. That way, it doesn't feel like work. It just feels like fun."[4]

BUILDING STRONGER BONES

Just as in strengthening muscles, stress is the key to building stronger bones. Exercises such as lifting weights, using resistance bands, and performing push-ups put pressure on a body's bones. The body responds by activating bone-forming cells to increase the body's bone density. Humans build most of their bone density as children and teens, so strengthening bones from a young age is a good way to avoid bone weakness and injuries as an adult. A healthy diet that includes ample calcium and vitamin D also supports growing bones.

STRENGTH TRAINING BENEFITS

Many health experts agree that making strength training fun is key to keeping youth interested in these activities. One recommendation is to change workout routines regularly to avoid boredom. Health experts want youth to stay interested not only so they can enjoy the benefits of strength training in adolescence but also so they can learn how to help their bodies stay strong throughout their adulthood.

The CDC has fitness guidelines for adults. These guidelines recommend at least two days per week of strength training exercises that work all major muscle groups.[5] The organization says adults should work to the point at which another repetition of a set of exercises would be difficult.

The CDC also encourages adults to gradually increase the amount of weight they use or the number of days they strength train in order to keep building stronger muscles. Recommendations for strength training exercises include lifting weights. However, experts also recommend body-weight exercises such as push-ups, using resistance bands, and climbing stairs.

The guidelines note that even adults ages 65 and older can follow these same recommendations as long as they are active and healthy. Strength training has several benefits for both teens and adults. These benefits include healthier bones, improved cognition, reduced symptoms of depression, and a lower risk of health issues as they age.

Studies show that strength training can reduce anxiety.

Organizations such as the National Strength and Conditioning Association (NSCA) agree that the goal of youth strength training should be building a foundation for a lifetime of healthy physical activity. In 2020, the NSCA published an article titled "Kids Must Strength Train–A Call to Action." In the paper, the organization noted that as a society Americans are getting more inactive and urged adults to lead by example to get their kids interested in strength training.

The NSCA touted the physical benefits of youth strength training, such as a decreased chance of childhood diabetes. The organization said strength training has also been shown to improve sleep quality, brain health, and emotional and mental well-being in young people.

Many young athletes had entire seasons canceled due to the COVID-19 pandemic.

In its paper, the NSCA also said strength training plays an important role in helping youth avoid injury. The organization said children can get injured when their bodies are not used to the forces required for activities such as running, jumping, and changing direction. According to the NSCA, strength training prevents injuries by familiarizing the muscles, bones, and joints with the increased stress of these movements.

GAIN WITHOUT PAIN

NSCA released its paper in November 2020, amid the COVID-19 pandemic. During this time, many schools and community organizations suspended sports activities, resulting in a drop in many sports-related injuries. For example, the *Orthopaedic Journal of Sports Medicine* reported that youth emergency room visits related to a team sports injury decreased by 76.9 percent during the 2020 lockdown period.[6]

However, after youth organized sports resumed, some health experts reported an increase in stress fractures, muscle strains, and injuries to the knees, shoulders, and elbows. Many of the issues seemed to have been caused by athletes trying to ramp up too quickly to their previous levels of activity. Experts hypothesized that weakness resulting from the pandemic interruption may have contributed to these injuries, seemingly underscoring NSCA's point about youth inactivity and injuries.

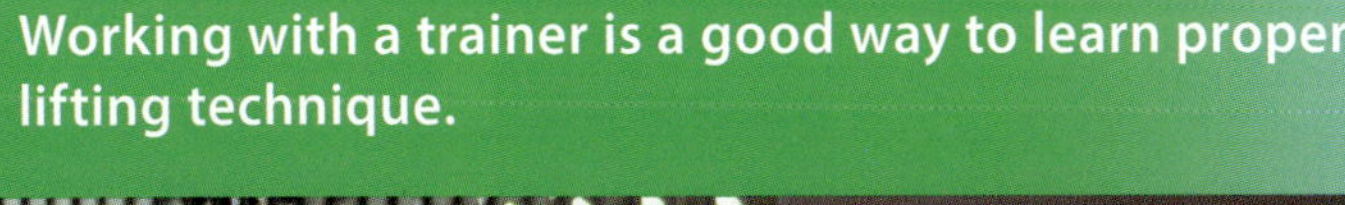

Working with a trainer is a good way to learn proper lifting technique.

STAYING HYDRATED

It's important to stay hydrated while strength training. Experts recommend drinking plain water during training sessions that are less than an hour. Sports drinks that are infused with electrolytes or vitamins are usually only needed for high levels of intense activity. Experts caution against consuming energy drinks that have caffeine, as these drinks don't replenish the body's nutrients. Failure to drink enough water can lead to dehydration. Symptoms of dehydration include thirst, fatigue, and muscle cramps. Severe dehydration can lead to fainting and heatstroke.

Health experts recommend that young people always begin a new strength training plan by gradually increasing activity levels in order to avoid injury. Young people should first try exercises without using weights, then complete one set of eight to 15 reps per session using a light weight before moving to heavier weights and more sets. Getting advice from qualified strength trainers about maintaining proper weight-lifting form is another way to avoid getting hurt.

Experts also recommend taking the time to warm up and cool down with aerobic activity and stretches before and after training sessions. Taking a rest day in between training sessions also gives tired muscles time to recover before the next workout. Fueling sessions with healthy meals is another key to strength training success.

Many coaches say strength training for youth athletes should focus on the whole body rather than on strengthening only one area. The trend of working

Following a set workout plan can help a person track progress and avoid injury.

out only one muscle group per session is also changing. However, for athletes focused on training specific muscle groups, experts advise performing varied exercises. This ensures that athletes continue to make progress and can prevent injuries from overusing muscles. Above all, strength training is individualized. For the best results, athletes can contact an expert to design the best strength training plan for their specific goals and lifestyle.

EASTON
USA
8

CHAPTER

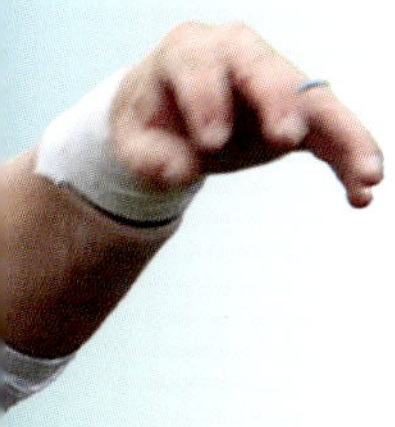

ARM STRENGTH

Haylie McCleney grew up dreaming of being an Olympic softball player. She played as an outfielder for her local softball team and was always the smallest kid on the field. In high school, she started lifting weights to build more muscle. She credits her weight-lifting routine with helping her earn a scholarship to the University of Alabama softball team. In 2013, at just 19 years old, McCleney joined the US Women's National Team.

McCleney's Olympic dreams came true in 2021 at the Tokyo Games. McCleney continues to play softball professionally for the Athletes Unlimited league. She also shares arm strength training tips on social media. She encourages her followers to warm up before games with certain arm strengthening exercises that use resistance bands.

Haylie McCleney was the starting center fielder for the United States softball team at the Tokyo Olympic Games.

"[Resistance band work] has been a game changer for me in my career," McCleney posted on Instagram in 2023. "I do this every single time I go to throw, and my arm feels more fresh than ever."[1]

ARM STRENGTHENING EXERCISES

Softball and baseball players need tremendous arm strength. However, nonathletes can also benefit from arm strength training. Arm strength training improves the range of motion in the arms by strengthening the forearms, biceps, and triceps. This training also helps keep shoulder joints stable by strengthening the muscles in the arms and shoulders.

Most arm exercises should be performed in sets of eight to 12 reps. Experts have found that this is the optimal range for building muscle, but you may need to modify the exercise. If you can't perform eight reps, the exercise is too difficult

STRENGTH TRAINING FOR BREAKDANCING

Breakdancers are also known as breakers. Their routines can include spinning with their whole bodies on their hands, heads, or shoulders. These gravity-defying moves require great strength, flexibility, and balance. Breakers strengthened their bodies to prepare to compete at the 2024 Olympics. Breaker Karam Singh trained on his own by doing body-weight exercises such as sit-ups, push-ups, and pull-ups. Breaker India Sardjoe worked with a strength and conditioning trainer to get ready.

and may need modification. If you can perform more than 12 reps before reaching the point that you can't complete another rep, the exercise is too easy. You can increase difficulty by adding more resistance or by changing how you move, such as holding a halfway position of a rep for a few seconds. For exercises that use weights, you can add or decrease the weight being lifted until you're performing the right amount of reps.

It is also important to rest your arms in between sets to avoid overworking your muscles. Pain, tingling, or numbness in your hands, arms, or neck after exercising may be signs of an injury. Check with an expert before returning to strength training.

Baseball and softball pitchers often warm up with bands to help prevent elbow and shoulder injuries.

AI IN THE WEIGHT ROOM

The term *artificial intelligence* (AI) was coined in the 1950s. AI refers to the ability of a computer or software to perform complex tasks that are typically associated with human intelligence. Although AI is not new, people keep finding new ways to use it, and strength training is no exception. Several college football coaches use an AI weight training program from the fitness tech company Perch to track players' workouts.

Jacob Rothman, a former Massachusetts Institute of Technology baseball player, founded Perch in 2016. After herniating a disc in his back while lifting weights, Rothman envisioned a "smart gym" that could alert athletes to overexertion so they could avoid the risk of injury. Perch now works with ex-athletes, coaches, fitness experts, and tech wizards to create weight room machines that use AI and 3D camera technology to provide feedback on performance.

The University of Georgia football

Smart fitness machines have changed the way many people exercise.

team uses a Perch system in its weight room. Known as the "DawgTron," the machine's massive digital screen displays the players' lifting stats. "Our players now see who's moving the bar the fastest," said Scott Sinclair, the team's lead strength and conditioning coach.[2]

Aly Orady, a supercomputer engineer, is the founder of another AI strength training company called Tonal. His company makes an AI weight machine that provides personalized feedback on lifters' form, safe levels of resistance for each lifter, and coach-led workouts to help people make progress while lifting correctly.

BICEPS CURL

Lift until weights meet shoulders

Keep shoulders down and back, and chest open

Bend at elbows to start curling

Keep elbows by sides

Stand with feet hip-width apart

BICEPS CURL AND TRICEPS EXTENSION

Curls target the biceps muscle. They are located on the front of your upper arm. Improving these muscles can lead to benefits such as better ball-handling skills in basketball or more easily lifting heavy objects.

To perform a double-arm curl, pick up a pair of dumbbells and stand with your feet hip-width apart. Lower your arms to your sides while keeping your palms facing upward. Bend your elbows and slowly lift the weights until they are near your shoulders. Make sure your wrists don't bend throughout the exercise. Then lower the weights back down to the starting position. A biceps curl can be performed using each arm individually or both arms at once. When curling individually, make sure you perform the same number of reps with each arm.

The triceps extension helps stabilize the muscles in your shoulders. Pick up a dumbbell and stand with your feet shoulder-width apart. Then use both hands to raise the dumbbell above

STRENGTH TRAINING FOR ARM WRESTLING

Croatian Rino Mašić started studying arm wrestling as a teenager by watching videos on YouTube. At age 14, Mašić started his own training program to become a competitive arm wrestler. He went on to win several titles, including the 2022 junior world title at age 17. Now, Mašić posts arm strength training exercises on his TikTok channel to help others build muscle.

your head. Slowly bend your elbows to lower the weight behind your head, keeping your core muscles tight and your elbows pointing up and not out. Finish the move by lifting the weight back to the starting position.

SINGLE-ARM BENCH PRESS

The single-arm bench press works the muscles of the chest, shoulders, and triceps. It is meant to improve the muscular balance in both arms. To perform a set, you will need a workout bench and two dumbbells. A workout bench allows for a greater range of motion, but this exercise can also be done on the floor.

Start with a dumbbell in each hand and lie down with your back on the bench or floor. Lift both dumbbells over your chest and keep your palms facing each other at about a 45-degree angle. Squeeze your shoulders together, then bend your elbow to lower one dumbbell until it touches

PATRICK MAHOMES

Kansas City Chiefs quarterback Patrick Mahomes may be a football star, but Mahomes credits baseball with helping him build his arm and shoulder strength. He grew up practicing long tosses with his father, who was a major league pitcher. This drill involves gradually backing up as you toss a ball to a partner. Mahomes continues using this drill with a football before every game. "That is strictly from baseball," Mahomes said. "To me, until I get those long tosses in, I haven't loosened up my arm."[3]

Triceps extensions can be performed while standing, kneeling, or lying down on the floor or a weight bench.

the side of your chest or your elbow touches the floor. Your bent arm should be at a 45-degree angle from your shoulder, rather than straight out to the side. After holding it there for a second, push the dumbbell back up to the starting position. Repeat that motion for the desired number of reps. You can either complete all reps with one arm first or alternate arms until the set is complete.

SINGLE-ARM DUMBBELL ROW

Single-arm rows target the shoulders and upper back. The movement is often used by football quarterbacks and baseball pitchers to counterbalance the pushing motions made by throwing. You will need one dumbbell and a

FITNESS SNAPSHOT

SINGLE-ARM DUMBBELL ROW

workout bench to perform this exercise. You can also do this exercise on the floor on your hands and knees.

Pick up the dumbbell with one hand, with your palm facing your side. Place your opposite knee on the bench while leaning forward with the weight hanging down at about knee height. Your upper body should be parallel to the floor. Place your free hand on the bench to hold you up.

Squeeze your back muscles together and pull the dumbbell up to your side between your ribs and hips. Do not shrug your shoulder up toward your ears. Hold at the top of the motion for one second, then carefully lower the weight back down to complete one rep. Repeat for the desired number of reps before switching to the other arm.

CHIN-UP AND PULL-UP

Chin-ups and pull-ups look very similar. Both are body-weight exercises where you use a bar to hoist yourself up. However, one small adjustment allows each exercise to target different muscles. Chin-ups are done by gripping the bar with your palms facing toward you. This is called a supinated grip. Chin-ups primarily work the biceps and pectoral muscles. Pull-ups are done by gripping the bar with your palms facing away from you, which is called a pronated grip. The lifting motion of a pull-up works the latissimus dorsi and trapezius muscles.

To perform either exercise, grab the bar in the appropriate way. Keep your hands slightly narrower than the width of your shoulders. Squeeze your shoulder blades together and tighten your core. Pull your elbows down as you lift yourself up. The goal is to get your chin over the bar. Try to keep your legs straight and avoid swinging them as you lift. Repeat until you are unable to pull yourself up to start another rep.

SHOULDER ROTATION

Rotations can be done in multiple ways. Both internal and external rotations target your shoulder's rotator cuff. They can both prevent shoulder injuries and increase throwing power.

To perform an internal rotation, lie on your back with your knees bent. Pick up a dumbbell in one hand while propping your elbow on the floor next to your body. Bend the arm at a 90-degree angle. Without lifting your elbow from the floor, slowly lower your forearm toward the ground. Stop before you reach the floor, then slowly bring your arm back to the starting position. Repeat for the desired number of reps before switching to the other arm.

For an external rotation, sit on the floor with your right leg extended. Bend the left knee up toward the chest, and place that foot flat on the ground with your right hand on the floor for support. Holding a dumbbell in your left

Chin-ups and pull-ups work the same muscles. The only difference is which muscles will be working harder while using the different grips.

hand, bend your arm at a 90-degree angle and rest your elbow on your bent left knee. Your arm should be vertical, and your palm should be facing the right.

Without moving your elbow off your knee, slowly lower the dumbbell toward you until your forearm is parallel to the floor. Hold the position for two to three seconds, then slowly lift your arm to the starting position. Repeat and switch to the other arm.

CHAPTER

CHEST STRENGTH

While Tiger Woods was dominating professional golf in the late 1990s and into the 2000s, he set a new standard for strength training in professional golf. Yet star golfer Rory McIlroy, who broke into the pro ranks in 2007 at age 18, didn't think much about going to the gym until his back started hurting in his early twenties.

The four-time major champion started a strength training program that has helped him stay at the top of his game. In 2023, McIlroy was ranked the No. 2 player in the world, with a driver swing speed of 122 miles per hour (196 kmh) and an average driving distance of 326 yards (298 m).[1]

Although McIlroy works out regularly, including during golf competitions, he has no plans to lift big weights like a bodybuilder. He says strength

Tiger Woods, *left*, and Rory McIlroy, *right*, have a combined 19 victories in major golf tournaments.

STEPH CURRY

To stay strong, Golden State Warriors point guard Steph Curry does an intense drill called a full-court star. During the drill, Curry challenges himself to make at least eight of ten shot attempts in 55 seconds, running to the opposite end of the court between each shot. Curry also practices weight lifting and can deadlift 400 pounds (180 kg).[3] Warriors coach Steve Kerr credits strength training for Curry's stamina, strong defense, and fluid movements. "The guy is amazing," Kerr said. "He just keeps working on his game, his strength, his conditioning, year after year."[4]

training has helped him meet his goal of controlling his club all the way through his swing. His upper-body strength training regimen includes medicine ball throws, chest presses, jumps, squats, dead lifts, pull-ups, and chin-ups.

McIlroy says his workouts have helped him both physically and mentally. "My posture was terrible when I started," he said. "To have better posture, to stand up straight with your shoulders back and your chest out, it even just gives off the air of confidence."[2]

CHEST STRENGTHENING EXERCISES

Golf is just one sport that requires a great deal of chest and upper body strength. However, everyone can benefit from chest strength training. This can help people improve their posture and arm mobility, both of which are useful in everyday life.

Many people warm up or stretch with bands before starting a strength training workout.

Be sure to include stretches in your workout, such as the horizontal arm extension. To do this stretch, start by holding your arms straight out in front of you with your palms facing down or forward. Then, keeping your arms straight, extend them to the sides, forming a T-shape with your body. Hold your arms out for one second before returning to your starting position. Repeat this stretch for the desired number of repetitions.

PUSH-UP

Push-ups focus on the abdominal, arm, and chest muscles. They can be done either on the floor or on an exercise mat. The benefits include shoulder injury prevention, as well as improved posture and balance.

Lie face down, then push yourself up so you are resting on your hands and toes and your body is in a straight line. Straighten your arms, but do not lock your elbows. Your hands should be below your shoulders and your legs should be about one foot (30.5 cm) apart.

Tighten your core muscles to keep your body in a straight line as you lower yourself toward the ground by bending your elbows. Your elbows should be angled about 45 degrees away from your body, not straight out to the side. Stop before your chest touches the ground. Keep your core muscles tight as you push back up toward the starting position.

Push-ups can be modified by performing the movement at an incline or on the knees.

DUMBBELL PULLOVER

Dumbbell pullovers will target the muscles in your chest and back, specifically in the shoulder blade area. To perform them, you will need a workout bench and a dumbbell. However, this exercise can also be done lying on the floor. Sit on one end of the bench, placing your feet flat on the floor. Without moving your feet, lie on your back so that your head is at one end of the bench, with both your head and neck supported.

Hold the dumbbell in both hands above your chest, arms extended, keeping your palms facing each other. Tighten your back and core muscles, then slowly lower the weight behind your head as low as you can with your arms still fully extended. Move with control so that this part takes about three to four seconds. Then slowly lift the weight back up to the starting position above your chest. That is one rep. Repeat for the desired number of reps.

BENCH PRESS

The bench press is another exercise that targets the arm and chest muscles. In addition to increasing strength, it also increases endurance. You will need a workout bench, but you can do the exercise on the floor, using two dumbbells or a dedicated bench press rack with a barbell.

With your feet firmly on the floor, lie on your back, supported by the bench. Hold the dumbbells above your

Dumbbell pullovers need to be performed with a stable spine. Performing the exercise correctly can help build better posture.

chest with your arms held slightly wider than shoulder width. Keep your hips on the bench and your core muscles tight as you bend your elbows to lower the dumbbells toward your chest.

As with a push-up, make sure your bent arms are at a 45-degree angle from your shoulders. Stop lowering the dumbbells when your elbows are just below the bench or they meet the floor. Then, pull your shoulder blades together, brace your core, and push the dumbbells back up to the starting position. Repeat for the desired number of reps and sets, but make sure to rest between sets.

MARCHING BANDS

Playing in a marching band requires strength, flexibility, endurance, and cardiovascular conditioning. In marching bands, musicians march at fast speeds while holding instruments that can weigh up to 40 pounds (18 kg) and blowing air through those instruments for up to 12 minutes. To get ready for game day or a marching band competition, coaches recommend that band members incorporate running, calf raises, push-ups, sit-ups, and planks into their strength training routines.

BENCH DIP

Bench dips target the triceps and the upper back and also work the chest. They can be done on a dedicated workout bench. However, if you do not have one, you can substitute any stable chair or bench of a similar height.

Sit on the bench and place your palms down next to your thighs, fingers facing forward. Extend your legs and

Dumbbell bench presses can be performed on a flat or an inclined bench to target different muscles.

hold yourself over the bench with extended arms. Your spine should be straight and neutral. Keeping your elbows in, lower your body until your arms are at 90-degree angles. Use your palms to push yourself back up to the starting position to complete one rep. Throughout the exercise, keep your shoulders down and away from your ears and avoid sinking into them. If performing the dip with straight legs is too challenging, feel free to bend your knees and bring your feet closer to your body.

MEDICINE BALL EXERCISES

A medicine ball chest press targets several upper body muscles, including the chest, core, and shoulders. To begin, pick up the medicine ball and stand with your

FITNESS SNAPSHOT

BENCH DIP

FITNESS SNAPSHOT

MEDICINE BALL THROW

Throw ball up and against the wall

Fully extend arms when throwing

Begin movement with ball at chest before extending upward

Keep feet hip-width apart

feet hip-width apart. Hold the ball in front of your chest with your elbows bent at 90-degree angles.

Roll your shoulders back and down, then slowly push the medicine ball out in front of you. Don't stop until you have fully straightened your arms. Then pull the ball back to your chest to complete one rep. This move can also be done by holding a dumbbell by the sides.

A medicine ball throw targets the arms and upper back. You will need a medicine ball, as well as a wall with enough open space above and on either side of you. As with the chest press, begin with your feet hip-width apart, the ball held in front of you, and your elbows bent at 90-degree angles. Raise the ball over your head until your arms are fully extended. Then throw the ball against the wall. Retrieve the ball and begin again.

FUELING WITH FOOD

Health experts agree that the best way to boost athletic performance is to maintain a healthy diet. The US Department of Agriculture (USDA) provides tips on healthy eating. It recommends that youth and teens include fruits, vegetables, whole grains, and proteins in their meals. The USDA encourages people to eat a variety of proteins, such as seafood, eggs, lentils, beans, nuts, milk, or soy products, in addition to meat and poultry. Eating healthy is especially important for young athletes on game days. Experts encourage athletes to eat breakfast and reload with food and fluids soon after their competition ends.

JAX
94

CHAPTER SIX

CORE STRENGTH

Cassie Ettel grew up watching football with her mom. Inspired by her mother's passion for the sport, Cassie decided to pursue a career in the National Football League (NFL). That dream came true in 2019. That year, Ettel became the associate athletic trainer for the Jacksonville Jaguars. In 2023, she was one of just 21 female athletic trainers in the NFL.[1]

Ettel says a strong, stable core is the key to both injury prevention and power for football players. Her core strength training program for the Jaguars focuses not only on the abdominals but on the muscles along the sides of the torso, pelvis, and spine as well. Ettel's workouts include exercises such as dead bugs, bird dogs, in and outs, and diagonal crunches. Her goal is to help players

Athletic trainers for NFL teams focus on core strength, which can help improve players' movement and prevent injuries.

increase their strength, balance, and power, all while avoiding injuries.

"The core plays a vital role in the body's mechanics and athletic performance," Ettel said. "It's the link between the upper and lower body and forms the foundational support for all movements of the limbs. Trying to generate power from a weak core is like trying to build a house on a foundation of sand."[2]

KATIE LEDECKY

In 2023, Katie Ledecky broke Michael Phelps's record for the most individual swimming world titles. She earned her sixteenth world title at the World Aquatic Championships in Japan by winning the 800-meter freestyle with a time of 8:08:87.[3] Ledecky, who has also won seven Olympic gold medals, includes core strengthening exercises such as chin-ups, pull-ups, squats, and dead lifts in her workout routine. "I think core strength is incredibly important in swimming—it's that connecting piece between your arms and legs," Ledecky said.[4]

CORE STRENGTHENING EXERCISES

Football players rely on core strength to throw perfect passes or to tackle players without tiring. However, both athletes and nonathletes can benefit from core strength training. People need a strong, stable core to perform everyday activities, such as walking and picking up items.

During core workouts, be sure to include stretches such as the cat-cow. To do this stretch, position yourself

Sit-ups can be performed in many different ways. Experts suggest starting with three sets of ten to 15 sit-ups per day if you are new to exercising.

on all fours on a mat with your knees below your hips and hands below your shoulders. Start by arching your spine up like a cat, then push your abdominals toward the floor and your chest up to stretch your abs.

SIT-UP

Sit-ups not only improve your core strength but also your posture. They can also help prevent back injuries. To begin, lie down with your back on the exercise mat.

FITNESS SNAPSHOT

PLANK

Bend your knees and plant your feet firmly on the floor. Position your arms either crossed over on your chest or held up with your hands touching the sides of your head.

Without moving your lower body, tighten your abdominal muscles and use them to lift your upper back off the ground. Keep rising until you are in a sitting position. Then, slowly lower yourself back to your starting position while keeping your abdominal muscles tight. Your lower back should not arch forward at any point.

CONNOR MCDAVID

National Hockey League star Connor McDavid is known for both his speed on the ice and his scoring ability. The Edmonton Oilers center's top speed is about 25 miles per hour (40 kmh).[5] In the 2022–23 season, McDavid tallied 153 points, with 64 goals and 89 assists. It was the highest scoring NHL season by any player in 28 years.[6] McDavid has shared core strengthening exercises on his social media to help other hockey players improve. His routine includes squats, push-ups, lunges, planks, and box jumps.

PLANK

A plank not only works your core muscles but also benefits the upper and lower body. Begin by lying face down on the mat. With your hands under your shoulders, place your palms firmly on the mat and push yourself up on your hands and toes. Keep your arms and legs straight, with your feet hip-width apart.

Tighten your core muscles, and make sure your body stays in a straight line from your head to your feet. Hold this pose for the desired length of time. Beginners should start with a short interval of roughly 15 to 20 seconds. You can also do a plank on your knees, still making sure the whole body is aligned. Stop when you are no longer able to hold proper form. You can begin to add more time as your body gets stronger and more comfortable in the pose. You can also mix up the exercise by resting your upper body on your elbows and forearms instead of your hands.

SUPERMAN

The superman is great for the upper back and also works the lower back and gluteus muscles. It is a good exercise to prevent injuries and improve posture. Start by lying face down on the mat. Extend your arms straight out in front of you and your legs straight back.

Slowly lift your arms and legs at the same time until you feel your lower back muscles contract. Keep your head in a neutral position while you pull your shoulder blades together and tighten your core and gluteus muscles. Be sure not to shrug your shoulders. Hold this position for two to three seconds. Lower your arms, legs, and belly back to the mat to complete one rep. Aim for three sets of eight to 12 reps each.

FITNESS SNAPSHOT

SUPERMAN

The bird dog exercise is also called a quadruped reach or simply the quadruped.

DEAD BUG

The dead bug is a great exercise for stabilizing your arms and legs while they are moving. To begin, lie with your back flat on the mat. Hold your legs up with your knees bent at a 90-degree angle. Raise your arms straight up. Keep your wrists above your shoulders.

Slowly move your right arm backward toward the ground. At the same time, extend your left leg toward the floor. When your limbs are parallel to the ground, return both limbs to the starting position. Make sure your lower back stays flat on the ground throughout, even if it means you don't get your limbs parallel to the ground. Repeat that motion, but this time lower your left arm and right leg together.

BIRD DOG

The bird dog is a simple exercise that helps stabilize your arms and legs and improve your posture. The exercise targets your abdominals, gluteus, and lower back muscles. Bird dogs can be done on the floor but are more comfortable when using a soft exercise mat.

Start with your palms and knees on the mat. Slowly move your right arm straight out in front of you. At the same time, extend your left leg behind you. Keep your arm in line with your head and your back flat. Keep your leg in line with your hip, your hips level, and your back flat. Return your limbs to their starting positions and repeat with your left arm and right leg.

STRENGTH TRAINING ON GAME DAY?

Should young athletes lift weights on game day? It's a question that has long been up for debate. Some coaches and parents are concerned that working out on a game day could cause athletes to use up energy that they might need during the game. But some coaches say weight lifting on game day can actually improve performance and power as long as athletes aren't training until they're fatigued. Others say it's OK for athletes to train earlier in the day, especially since it might help alleviate game-day anxiety.

PLANK IN AND OUT

There are several ways to add more challenge to a traditional plank. To perform a plank in and out, start by lying face down on the mat. Push yourself up into plank position with your flat palms so you are supported by your hands and toes. Keep your arms and legs straight, with your feet hip-width apart.

Without moving your hands, jump and pull your legs forward, landing on your toes with your knees between your arms and your feet under your waist. Keep your head in a neutral position. Jump again, landing back in a strong plank with your feet back in their starting position. Steadily increase your speed with each rep as you repeat the set.

DIAGONAL CRUNCH

A diagonal crunch works your oblique muscles, which are located on the sides of your body. They are designed to stabilize your body when you are performing an activity that involves rotation. A diagonal crunch can be done on an exercise mat or a comfortable spot on the floor. They can also be done while holding a weight for an additional challenge.

Start by lying down on the floor or mat. Touch your fingertips to the sides of your head, with your elbows pointing out to your sides. Bend your knees so your feet are flat on the floor, then bring your left leg up. You can either hold it in the air with your knee bent at a 90-degree angle or rest your left ankle on your right knee in a figure-four position. Rise by bringing your upper back off

Diagonal crunches can be adapted to suit each exerciser's needs.

the floor in a controlled manner. Continue this motion while twisting your body and attempt to touch your right elbow to your left knee. Lower yourself back to the floor. Complete the desired number of reps, then switch the position of your legs and repeat on the opposite side.

USA
TDK
LYLES
BUDAPEST23

CHAPTER SEVEN

LEG STRENGTH

When Olympic sprinting legend Usain Bolt retired in 2017, he still held the world record for the 200-meter sprint with a time of 19.19 seconds.[1] Noah Lyles was 12 when Bolt set the world record. At 15, Lyles switched from competing as a high jumper to become a sprinter. He excelled in the short races, winning his first world title in the 200-meter race in 2019.

Three years later, at age 25, Lyles won the world title again, and in the process broke the American 200-meter record by one-hundredth of a second with a time of 19.31 seconds.[2] Before the 2023 world championships, Lyles said he hoped to break Bolt's world record in the 200. Though Lyles fell just shy of that, he did join Bolt in an elite group of

Noah Lyles waves to fans after helping the United States 4x100-meter relay team win gold at the 2023 world championships.

High knees are one of many warm-up exercises for the legs.

athletes to win the 100- and 200-meter sprints at the same world championships.

Lyles shares his favorite exercises on social media to help others become better sprinters. His leg strength training routine includes a variety of hops, skips, and taps while running. He also does plyometric box jumps, squats, dead lifts, and step-ups. Lyles is confident that with continued work, he will someday beat Bolt's 200-meter record. "I know that I'm going to break it," he said.[3]

LEG STRENGTHENING EXERCISES

While track-and-field athletes need to have enough power to sprint at high speeds, leap over hurdles, and launch themselves into the air for the long jump or pole vault competitions, everyone can benefit from leg strength training. Strengthening legs has been shown to improve balance and bone density. Both of these benefits are important for leading a healthy life.

Before beginning strength training exercises, start with warm-up exercises such as A-skips. To do A-skips, raise your right arm and left leg as you skip, then repeat with the other leg. High knees are another great warm-up exercise. To do high knees, bring your knees up high into the air in front of you as you run and swing your arms to propel yourself forward.

MISTY COPELAND

In 2015, Misty Copeland became the first Black female principal dancer at the American Ballet Theatre. She took a break from ballet in 2022 to have her son but later resumed training in hopes of returning to the stage. Her workout routine includes 40 calf raises and wearing light weights on her ankles for inner thigh strengthening exercises. When she's performing, Copeland rehearses for seven to nine hours every day. "This isn't a long career, so it's really important to stay in tip-top shape and never stop dancing," Copeland said.[4]

FITNESS SNAPSHOT

SQUAT

Keep head neutral

If needed, keep arms out for balance

Keep back straight

Keep knees over toes

Sit as low as possible while maintaining form

Keep weight toward heels

Keep feet shoulder-width apart

SQUAT

Squats are a valuable and adaptable exercise. They can be done either as a body-weight exercise or with weights. Squats improve mobility and strengthen bones while also targeting the calf, gluteus, and quadriceps muscles.

Start by standing with your feet at least shoulder-width apart. If using weights, hold a dumbbell in each hand, holding them down by your sides. You can also hold one or two dumbbells in front of your hips. Point your feet forward with your knees over your toes. Bend your knees and lower your hips back and down toward the floor, as if you were sitting.

Keeping your head neutral and your back straight, lower your hips back and down as far as you can. Make sure you maintain proper form throughout the exercise. It's important to brace your core and keep your chest open so your back doesn't round, especially if you are using weights. Also, your knees should point outward

MEGAN RAPINOE

In 2023, soccer legend Megan Rapinoe announced that she planned to retire later that year. During Rapinoe's 17-year career, she helped her team win two Women's World Cups and two Olympic medals. Her 73 assists were tied for third all-time among US Women's National Team players. Her 63 goals ranked tenth.[5] Rapinoe has credited strength training for helping her stay strong and powerful while running for 90 minutes or more during every game. Her workout routine includes yoga, Pilates, weight lifting, and using resistance bands.

rather than caving inward as you lower. Complete each rep by straightening your legs and simultaneously pushing your hips forward to return to the starting position.

LUNGE

Lunges can be done in any open space, either on the floor or on an exercise mat. They are great for targeting your calf, gluteus, and quadriceps muscles. In addition to improving jumping and sprinting ability, they are an excellent exercise for those seeking to increase flexibility.

Start with your feet hip-width apart. Take a step forward with your right leg while keeping your left foot in place. Your feet should still be hip-width apart, not directly in line with each other. Bend your legs at 90-degree angles, pushing into the mat with your right foot and left toes. Lower your body straight down until your left leg is nearly touching the mat. Push off your right foot and rise back up to your starting position, feet beside each other. You can do the desired number of reps all on one leg before switching, or you can alternate legs.

BRIDGE

Bridges can be done a few ways. They can be a static exercise, where you can hold the bridge pose for a set length of time. But they can also be done as a movement exercise, where you complete a set of lifts off the floor.

FITNESS SNAPSHOT

LUNGE

A bridge is one of many strength exercises influenced by the practice of yoga.

Both versions target the glutes and hamstrings and are excellent for improving stability and posture.

For a static bridge, lie down with your back on an exercise mat. Bend your knees and plant your feet firmly on the floor, hip-width apart, while resting your hands at your sides with your palms on the floor. Brace your core and raise your hips off the ground while squeezing your glutes together. Make sure your knees don't cave in toward each other, and do not arch the lower back. Keep your glutes and core tight as you hold this position for a desired length of time, then lower your hips back to their starting position. To make this a moving exercise, hold at the top for about two or three seconds, then lower your hips back to the ground to complete one rep.

PLYOMETRICS TRAINING

Plyometrics are hopping and skipping exercises. These exercises can include hopping onto a foam box or skipping along a track. Plyometrics help athletes have more control when they land after a jump and train them to be able to take off again quickly. Basketball, football, and soccer players are among the athletes who do plyometrics to gain power. Basketball star LeBron James has incorporated plyometrics into his training routine to stay strong. His workout exercises include jump squats, push hops, skipping, and stair climbing.

SINGLE-LEG DEAD LIFT

Dead lifts target your gluteus and hamstring muscles and also increase your balance and mobility. To begin a single-leg dead lift, place a dumbbell on the floor in front of your mat. Stand up straight on the mat with your left hand hanging down in front of you. Place your right hand on your right hip, or hold your right arm out to the side for balance.

This kind of dead lift uses a hinging motion at the hips, so your back and the leg you're balancing on must be straight the whole time. Push your hips backward, placing all the weight in your right heel, and lean your chest down. At the same time, lift your extended left leg behind you, keeping it in line with your torso.

When your chest is about parallel to the floor, pick up the dumbbell with your left hand, but do not round the back or twist your torso to do so. Use your hamstrings in your right leg to push your hips forward, squeezing your glutes together to straighten back to standing. Let your left arm hang as your torso lifts back up, and remember to keep your back straight. The dumbbell should end up in front of your left hip.

Place the dumbbell back on the floor, and repeat before switching sides. If lifting your leg off the ground is too challenging, you can leave that foot on the ground slightly behind you as you hinge, but make sure you keep all the weight in your working leg. Also, if you can't reach your arm to the floor without rounding your back, you can place the dumbbell on a low block or some books so it's a little higher off the ground.

SINGLE-LEG BOX JUMP

Single-leg box jumps are a great way to improve acceleration while strengthening your leg muscles. Start with a plyometric box one foot (30 cm) in front of you. Lift your left leg slightly behind you. Push your right foot into the floor and bend down as if squatting.

Raise both arms over your head as you prepare to jump, then lower them quickly as you propel yourself upward onto the box. Make sure you land on your right foot, with your knee soft. When you are finished, step down off the box and restart. You can either alternate legs or complete all reps on one side before switching.

Single-leg dead lifts can be performed with both free weights or kettlebells.

DOUBLE BOX JUMP

The double box jump is another excellent acceleration exercise. It also helps you practice proper jumping and landing techniques. To begin, you will need three plyometric boxes of different heights.

Start by sitting on the lowest box. Have a workout partner hold the tallest box steady on the ground. Push your legs into the floor, using the force to jump up to the second box. As soon as you land, jump again to the top box. Make sure to keep your knees and hips in a squat

When first performing box jumps, start with a lower box height and work up to using taller boxes.

position and your arms extended in front of you. When finished, climb down off the top box and return to your original seated position on the lowest box.

Double box jumps are often practiced by gymnasts as preparation for the vault apparatus.

MENTAL STRENGTH

Olympic gymnast Simone Biles is not only the most decorated athlete in gymnastics history. She is also one of several Olympic champions who have become mental health advocates. Biles withdrew from the team final at the Tokyo Olympic Games that took place in 2021. She cited the twisties, a loss of spatial awareness while in the air.

She turned the situation into an opportunity to discuss her mental health challenges and offer advice to youth athletes. "It's really important to use [your] support system," Biles later said. "We think we can do it on our own, but sometimes we just can't. So use every outlet given to you."[1]

Michael Phelps is another Olympic athlete who has opened up about the importance of mental health. He created the Michael Phelps

Simone Biles won two medals at the Tokyo Olympic Games and also made headlines for her stance on mental health during the competition.

Foundation, which promotes the idea that "good mental health is just as important as good physical health."[2] It's an idea that many coaches have embraced as they've seen the way good mental health can help improve an athlete's performance.

Many coaches see mental strength as an important part of overall strength training. They want their athletes to have the psychological skills to overcome both mental and physical challenges while competing. But mental strength is not solely about dealing with adversity. It's also about developing and maintaining a positive attitude.

People with a positive mindset tend to be more optimistic, motivated, and enthusiastic, which means they are more likely to reach their goals. Some experts argue that mental strength is what makes

MENTAL HEALTH ADVOCATES

One of the earliest Olympic athletes to discuss mental health was champion swimmer Michael Phelps. In 2015, Phelps disclosed his struggles with depression. In 2020, he joined other Olympic stars such as speed skater Apolo Anton Ohno and figure skater Sasha Cohen in the HBO documentary *The Weight of Gold*. The film, which Phelps coproduced, explores anxiety and depression among Olympic athletes. Phelps also speaks to young people about seeking help. "It all starts by realizing that it's OK not to feel OK and opening up," Phelps shared. "From there, anything's possible!"[3]

Having a calm mind can help athletes perform at their best.

Olympic athletes champions. They say that Olympic athletes often have more motivation, confidence, focus, and perceived social support. Fostering these skills can help people achieve their highest goals, whether or not they involve a gold medal.

MENTAL STRENGTHENING EXERCISES

Mental strength exercises can help you stay positive on your strength training journey. Keep your goals in mind and congratulate yourself for sticking with the steps needed to achieve them. However, it's also important to be patient with yourself when you fail or don't progress as quickly as you want.

Don't punish yourself by pushing through mental or physical pain just to prove that you're strong. Rest when you need to so you don't hurt yourself.

GETTING SOCIAL WITH STRENGTH TRAINING

Social media can be a source of information and inspiration for young athletes and other youth interested in strength training. But it also can provide misinformation or prompt feelings of insecurity when youth compare themselves to edited, unrealistic images of athletes and celebrities. Youth Football Online, a website created by a youth football coach and a football enthusiast, provides advice for youth athletes exploring social media.

Through the site they can follow high school and college coaches from all over the country and ask them questions online that will help promote useful discussion. They can also share information with other athletes. Examples include videos of training routines or exercises they and other young athletes may be interested in, or insights as to how they are improving their training or game-time performance.

It is important to research fitness influencers thoroughly before following their practices.

When using social media, it is important to interact in positive ways. Post and share uplifting stories and avoid those that are negative or untrue. Posting should be done in a smart way. People should avoid posting when they are upset, and they should share books, strategies, and other methods that fellow athletes might appreciate. Allowing only positive, goal-oriented people to participate will keep networks strong.

THE ROCK

Today Dwayne "The Rock" Johnson is a muscular action movie star, but the former professional wrestler did not start strength training for the muscles. He began weight lifting as a teenager to help deal with his difficult emotions after he and his family were evicted from their home. He credits strength training with helping him with his childhood depression.

If you are recovering from an injury, remember to take your training slow at first so you can return to your full activities without reinjuring yourself.

Although mental strength training exercises can help manage overwhelming emotions, they aren't a cure-all. Reach out to a trusted adult if you have symptoms of anxiety or depression. These symptoms can include negative feelings such as lingering sadness or fear as well as physical changes such as eating less than usual or an inability to sleep. In the same way that physical injuries sometimes require visits to a doctor, mental illnesses may require medicine or therapy. These tools can also be paired with mental strength training exercises to establish an even better mind-body connection.

DEEP BREATHING

Deep breathing is a soothing way to end an exercise session. It can also be a stand-alone activity to enhance mental strength, focus, and relieve stress. While this exercise might be more comfortable lying on an exercise mat, it can be performed anywhere you have enough space to lie down.

Start by lying on your back. Put one hand over your stomach and your other hand on your chest. Count to five as you breathe in through your nose and feel your stomach rise. Make sure to pause for a moment at the end of each inhale. Count to five as you breathe out through your nose before pausing at the end of the exhale.

PROGRESSIVE MUSCLE RELAXATION

In addition to bolstering mental strength and focus, progressive muscle relaxation can also help with sore muscles after a workout. Sit down or lie with your back on your exercise mat. Breathe in and tense up the muscles of your feet. Hold for a moment, then relax your feet as you breathe out.

Breathe in and tense up your leg muscles. Hold for a moment, then relax your legs as you breathe out. Continue tensing and relaxing your muscles until you've reached your neck.

MINDFULNESS MEDITATION

Sit down or lie with your back on your exercise mat. Close your eyes and count slowly from one to 60. As you count, observe your breath without trying to change it. Pay attention to the feeling of air passing through your nose

FITNESS SNAPSHOT

MINDFULNESS MEDITATION

and notice how your stomach expands and contracts with each breath.

If your mind starts to wander, notice each thought, then let it go and bring your attention back to your breath. Try not to get distracted by additional thoughts. Keep bringing your attention back to your breath. Repeat this exercise for longer periods of time if desired.

POSITIVE VISUALIZATIONS AND MANTRAS

Set a timer for one minute. Sit or lie with your back on your exercise mat. Close your eyes, take a deep breath in, and then exhale.

Focus on either a positive mental image or a positive mantra. A positive image could be a mental picture of making a perfect play during a game. A mantra is a motivational phrase you repeat to yourself, such as, "I can do what I set my mind to."

SPORTS ANXIETY

The yips and choking are two conditions that athletes fear. The yips are a sudden, involuntary failure to perform a fundamental skill. The cause is not completely understood, but it could be due to a mental challenge or a physical issue. Choking, on the other hand, is when athletes fail to perform under pressure due to changes in their mental state. Sports psychologists help athletes work to overcome the yips and choking through relaxation and visual imagery techniques.

ESSENTIAL FACTS

What Is Strength Training?

- Strength training is any exercise that makes your muscles contract against some type of opposing force.
- Strength training can include weight-lifting exercises or body-weight exercises, such as sit-ups, that make you move your body against gravity.
- The goal of strength training is to increase and maintain muscle strength.
- Jack LaLanne was a fitness pioneer who popularized strength training for everyday people.
- There are more than 115,000 gyms and health clubs in the United States alone in which people practice strength training.

Benefits of Strength Training

- Builds stronger muscles and bones, which can help with both athletic and everyday activities.
- Improves flexibility and mobility.
- Reinforces major joints, which can reduce the risk of injury.
- Can improve sleep, which helps with physical recovery, cognitive function, and emotional and mental well-being.

Quote

"When I first started training, the simple goal was to improve 1 percent in each exercise. . . . When I was doing strength workouts, it would be one more pull-up, one more sit-up, one more press-up, and one more squat and barbell in the gym."

—Chris Nikic, first person with Down syndrome to complete an Ironman Triathlon

GLOSSARY

abdominals

The band of muscles that lines the walls of the trunk of the body.

aerobic

Physical exercise that uses oxygen to power the heart and muscles.

biceps

The large muscle on the front of the upper arm between the elbow and shoulder.

bone density

The mass of a person's bones, which indicates bone strength.

cardio

Relating to an exercise that increases a person's heart rate.

cardiovascular

Related to the heart and blood vessels.

charlatan

A person who claims to have knowledge that they do not possess.

cognition

The process of acquiring knowledge and understanding through thought and experience.

core

Muscles that stabilize the midsection of the body, including abdominal and back muscles.

pectorals

Muscles that connect the upper arm and shoulder bones to the front of the chest.

Pilates

A low-impact exercise developed by Joseph Pilates that involves mind-body exercises and strengthening a person's core.

rep

Short for repetition, a single execution of an exercise, such as one push-up.

stamina

The ability to perform physical exercise for an extended time.

triceps

The large muscle on the back of the upper arm between the elbow and shoulder.

yoga

A Hindu spiritual practice that has grown popular as a low-impact exercise involving stretching, breathing, and balancing.

ADDITIONAL RESOURCES

Selected Bibliography

Kilian, Jonathan, and Justin Kilian. "Kids Must Strength Train—A Call to Action." *Personal Training Quarterly*, Nov. 2020, nsca.com. Accessed 13 Oct. 2023.

Stricker, Paul R., et al. "Resistance Training for Children and Adolescents." *Pediatrics*, 1 June 2020, publications.aap.org. Accessed 13 Oct. 2023.

"Weight Room No Longer Off Limits to Kids." *Stanford Medicine Children's Health*, 2023, stanfordchildrens.org. Accessed 13 Oct. 2023.

Further Readings

Alston, Valerie R. *Confident, Calm, and Clutch: How to Build Confidence and Mental Toughness for Young Athletes Using Sports Psychology*. Alchemy, 2023.

Horne, Moses, and Troy Horne. *Mental Toughness for Young Athletes: Eight Proven 5-Minute Mindset Exercises for Kids and Teens Who Play Competitive Sports*. Buggily Group, 2021.

Morris, Rebecca. *Sports Training*. Abdo, 2025.

Online Resources

To learn more about strength training, please visit **abdobooklinks.com** or scan this QR code. These links are routinely monitored and updated to provide the most current information available.

More Information

For more information on this subject, contact or visit the following organizations:

International Youth Conditioning Association (IYCA)

1298 W Ann Arbor Trl.
Plymouth, MI 48170
iyca.org

The IYCA provides knowledge and skills to people who work in the youth sports and fitness industry around the world.

National Strength and Conditioning Association (NSCA)

1885 Bob Johnson Dr.
Colorado Springs, CO 80906
nsca.com

The NSCA is a nonprofit organization whose mission is to advance strength and conditioning coaches and sports scientists around the world. It also provides guidelines for youth strength training.

US Centers for Disease Control and Prevention (CDC)

1600 Clifton Rd.
Atlanta, GA 30329
cdc.gov

The CDC is the nation's public health protection agency. It also provides guidelines for youth physical fitness, including strength training.

SOURCE NOTES

Chapter 1. Sailing Strong

1. "Rental Boats: Opti." *Bow To Stern Boating*, n.d., bowtosternboating.com. Accessed 13 Feb. 2024.

2. "Sailors: Introduction to the 420." *420 Sailing*, n.d., 420sailing.org. Accessed 13 Feb. 2024.

Chapter 2. What Is Strength Training?

1. Steve Shaw. "64 Arnold Schwarzenegger Quotes on Bodybuilding, Motivation, & Success." *Muscle & Strength*, 16 Jan. 2013, muscleandstrength.com. Accessed 25 Jan. 2024.

2. "Gym, Health & Fitness Clubs in the US - Number of Businesses." *Ibis World*, 27 Nov. 2023, ibisworld.com. Accessed 25 Jan. 2024.

3. Natalia Mehlman Petrzela. *Fit Nation: The Gains and Pains of America's Exercise Obsession*. University of Chicago, 2022. 115–116.

4. Nathaniel Meyersohn. "Americans Have Changed the Way They Exercise. Here's How Gyms Are Adapting." *CNN*, 1 Mar. 2023, cnn.com. Accessed 25 Jan. 2024.

5. Mary O'Neill. "Jack LaLanne Had Biceps and Brains." *Investors Business Daily*, 23 Jan. 2012, investors.com. Accessed 25 Jan. 2024.

6. Roger "Rock" Lockridge. "Elaine LaLanne, at Age 97, Continues to Reshape Fitness and Aging." *Muscle & Fitness*, n.d., muscleandfitness.com. Accessed 25 Jan. 2024.

7. "Women Gaining Ground on the Field of Play and at the Top Table." *International Olympic Committee*, 10 Mar. 2020, olympics.com. Accessed 25 Jan. 2024.

8. Meyersohn, "Americans Have Changed the Way They Exercise."

9. Maia Pandey. "Strength Training Has Surged in Popularity. Studies Show It Brings Particular Health Benefits." *NBC News*, 25 July 2023, nbcnews.com. Accessed 13 Feb. 2024.

10. Meyersohn, "Americans Have Changed the Way They Exercise."

Chapter 3. Strength Training and the Body

1. "The Inspirational Story Behind Down Syndrome Ironman History Maker Chris Nikic." *Olympics*, n.d., olympics.com. Accessed 25 Jan. 2024.

2. Kelsie Smith. "A 21-Year-Old Man Has Made History as the First Person with Down Syndrome to Complete an Ironman Triathlon." *CNN*, 10 Nov. 2020, cnn.com. Accessed 25 Jan. 2024.

3. "Physical Activity Guidelines for Americans, 2nd Edition." *United States Department of Health and Human Services,* 2018, health.gov. Accessed 25 Jan. 2024.

4. "Move Your Way: Try Something Different." *YouTube*, uploaded by Office of Disease Prevention and Health Promotion, 28 Apr. 2021, youtube.com. Accessed 25 Jan. 2024.

5. "Physical Activity Guidelines for Americans - 2nd Edition."

6. Ramsey S. Sabbagh, et al. "Effect of the COVID-19 Pandemic on Sports-Related Injuries Evaluated in US Emergency Departments." *National Library of Medicine*, 22 Feb. 2022, ncbi.nlm.nih.gov. Accessed 25 Jan. 2024.

Chapter 4. Arm Strength

1. Haylie McCleney. "@hayliemac8." *Instagram*, n.d., instagram.com. Accessed 25 Jan. 2024.

2. Tom Friend. "How College Football's National Champion Georgia Bulldogs Are Leveraging Perch's 3D Camera in the Weight Room." *Sports Business Journal*, 9 May 2023, sportsbusinessjournal.com. Accessed 25 Jan. 2024.

3. Brandon Hall. "The Childhood Drill That Helped Pat Mahomes Build Superhuman Arm Strength." *Stack*, 2 Nov. 2021, stack.com. Accessed 25 Jan. 2024.

SOURCE NOTES CONTINUED

Chapter 5. Chest Strength

1. Chris Ryan. "Six Key Moves You Can Learn from Rory McIlroy." *Today's Golfer*, 1 Jun. 2023, todays-golfer.com. Accessed 25 Jan. 2024.

2. Maddy Lucier. "How Strength Training Changed Rory McIlroy's Game." *Stack*, 30 Mar. 2015, stack.com. Accessed 25 Jan. 2024.

3. James Herbert. "Steph Curry Can Deadlift 400 Pounds." *CBS Sports*, 6 Jun. 2015, cbssports.com. Accessed 25 Jan. 2024.

4. Scott Davis. "Stephen Curry May Be the Best-Conditioned Player in the NBA, and His Incredibly Demanding Workouts Show Why." *Business Insider*, 10 Jun. 2022, businessinsider.com. Accessed 25 Jan. 2024.

Chapter 6. Core Strength

1. Alexandra Pecharich. "These Alumnae Keep the Chiefs and the Eagles in Super Bowl Shape." *Florida International University News*, 10 Feb. 2023, fiu.edu. Accessed 25 Jan. 2024.

2. Jen Murphy. "The Core Workout That Keeps an NFL Team Running." *Wall Street Journal*, 31 Oct. 2020, wsj.com. Accessed 25 Jan. 2024.

3. Simrin Singh. "Katie Ledecky Breaks Michael Phelps' Record for Most Individual World Titles." *CBS News*, 29 July 2023, cbsnews.com. Accessed 25 Jan. 2024.

4. Megan Falk. "Katie Ledecky Reveals the Rituals That Helped Her Snatch 4 Medals at the Tokyo Olympics." *Shape*, 9 Aug. 2021, shape.com. Accessed 25 Jan. 2024.

5. Apoorva Behl. "'That's Crazy': Speed Comparison with Usain Bolt Left NHL Star Connor McDavid Stunned in 2020." *Essentially Sports*, 25 Feb. 2023, essentiallysports.com. Accessed 25 Jan. 2024.

6. Colin Horgan. "2023 Belongs to NHL Sorcerer Connor McDavid – 2024 and 2025 Probably Will Too." *Guardian*, 29 Mar. 2023, theguardian.com. Accessed 25 Jan. 2024.

Chapter 7. Leg Strength

1. Sarah Gearhart. "Noah Lyles Is Coming for Usain Bolt's World Record." *Outside Online*, 24 Aug. 2023, outsideonline.com. Accessed 25 Jan. 2024.

2. Tom Schad and Lindsay Schnell. "Noah Lyles Sets American Record to Win 200 Meter World Title, as US Sweeps Again." *USA Today*, 22 July 2022, usatoday.com. Accessed 25 Jan. 2024.

3. Shad and Schnell, "Noah Lyles Sets American Record."

4. Alexa Tucker. "The Simple Exercise Misty Copeland Does 40 Times Every Morning." *Self*, 22 Nov. 2017, self.com. Accessed 25 Jan. 2024.

5. Steph Yang. "After Painful World Cup Finish, Megan Rapinoe 'Feels Like It's the Right Time' to Walk Away." *Athletic*, 6 Aug. 2023, theathletic.com. Accessed 25 Jan. 2024.

Chapter 8. Mental Strength

1. Scott Bregman. "Exclusive! Simone Biles on Sparking Mental Health Conversation: 'We're Going through It Together.'" *Olympics*, 10 Oct. 2021, olympics.com. Accessed 25 Jan. 2024.

2. "Open Up." *Michael Phelps Foundation*, n.d., michaelphelpsfoundation.org. Accessed 25 Jan. 2024.

3. "Open Up."

INDEX

ABOUT THE AUTHOR

Sarah Roggio

Sarah Roggio is a graduate of Northwestern University's Medill School of Journalism. She lives in Chicago, Illinois, where she loves to go sailing with her husband on Lake Michigan. Her strength training routine includes body-weight exercises, walking, yoga, and meditation to prepare for the physical and mental challenges of sailing.